THE ART OF SELLING

Learn How to Build Trust, Increase Sales,
Drive Revenue and Create Customer for Life

PRADIP DAS

© Copyright 2024 - All rights reserved.

The content contained within this book may not be reproduced, duplicated, or transmitted without direct written permission from the author or the publisher. Under no circumstances will any blame or legal responsibility be held against the publisher, or author, for any damages, reparation, or monetary loss due to the information contained within this book. Either directly or indirectly.

Legal Notice:

This book is copyright protected. This book is only for personal use. You cannot amend, distribute, sell, use, quote or paraphrase any part, or the content within this book, without the consent of the author or publisher.

Disclaimer Notice:

Please note the information contained within this document is for educational and entertainment purposes only. All effort has been executed to present accurate, up to date, and reliable, complete information. No warranties of any kind are declared or implied. Readers acknowledge that the author is not engaging in the rendering of legal, financial, medical or professional advice. The content within this book has been derived from various sources. Please consult a licensed professional before attempting any techniques outlined in this book.

By reading this document, the reader agrees that under no circumstances is the author responsible for any losses, direct or indirect, which are incurred as a result of the use of information contained within this document, including, but not limited to, — errors, omissions, or inaccuracies.

Author Profile

Table of Contents

Table of Contents..4

About the Book...6

1. Profit Magic: Turning Pain Points to Profits 13
2. Authentic Boost: Your Sales Journey 18
3. EmoSelling: The Emotional Sales Ride 24
4. Relationship Gold: Beyond Transactions......... 34
5. Service Superhero: Exceptional Customer moments 38
6. Brand Charisma: Company First, Product Second 44
7. ShopJoy: Crafting a Playful Buying Adventure 48
8. Buyer Bliss: Mastering The Art of Persuasion . 52
9. Partner Power: Unexpected Brand Alliance.... 56
10. PersonaCraft: Tailoring Sales with Precision 66
11. Quality Quest: The Key to Longevity........... 73
12. Resistance Vanish: Making Sales Smooth ... 79
13. Believe & Sell: Your Personal Sales Magic .. 91
14. Exquisite Service: Where Excellence Reigns 95

15.	SellTales: Crafting Stories for Impact.........102	
16.	Surprise Delight: Winning Customer Hearts 108	
17.	Taste Test: Savor Before you Commit 114	
18.	Urgency Thrive: The Power of Now...........120	
19.	Sales Symphony: Harmonizing Value Exchange 126	
20.	Voice2Value: Transforming Feedback into Solutions 130	

Book Summary 135

Additional Disclaimer for "The Art of Selling"........138

Common vs. Unorthodox Sales Practices...............140

About the Book

Have you ever met a salesperson who made you feel empowered, truly understood, and genuinely excited about what they had to offer? Picture someone beyond the conventional stereotypes – not the pushy, fast-talking figure, but an individual with an almost magical ability to connect with you and understand your needs. If this sounds unfamiliar, get ready for a pleasant surprise because "The Art of Selling" breaks away from the ordinary sales manuals you've encountered.

Picture a vibrant room filled with vitality, where individuals are geared up for a formidable journey. These aren't just salespeople; they are warriors on the quest for substantial dreams and more significant paydays. However, there's a surprising turn to the tale – even though everyone aspires to taste success, only a handful truly achieve it. Why does this happen?

Many find themselves trapped in monotony, endlessly delivering the same pitch and achieving identical numbers year in and year out. They transform into robots, losing sight of the real magic: the ability to connect with others and make a meaningful impact. In the pursuit of wealth, they overlook the influence of a helping hand and a sincere smile.

But some break free. They see every sale as a story, a chance to understand needs and ignite possibilities. They don't fight for money, they fight for impact, for leaving positive footprints in the world. Money follows, not as the goal, but as a reward for their genuine connection.

So, the question is - are you ready to question your routine? Are you ready to connect, not just sell? The battlefield awaits, but it's about hearts, not just numbers. Choose your approach wisely, and you too can write your own success story.

This book dismantles the traditional image of the salesperson and offers a refreshingly unique perspective. Unlike many sales gurus who boast years of direct experience closing deals, the author enlightens a completely different perspective. His wisdom develops not from personal victories on the sales floor, but from over two and a half decades spent observing, analysing successful practitioners across diverse organizations. He goes into the strategies of iconic brands and the stories of everyday individuals who, despite lacking formal sales training, have woven their magic and achieved remarkable success.

But is this a book worth your time? Can someone who hasn't actively sold offer valuable insights into the art of sales? The answer is a resounding yes, and here's why:

Often, the best way to understand a complex system is to observe it from far. This author's lack of direct sales experience becomes his strength. Unburdened by industry biases and preconceived notions, he approaches the subject with a fresh perspective, dissecting its core principles with keen objectivity. He filters the noise of industry jargon and focuses on the fundamental human truths that drive successful selling, truths applicable to any endeavor where persuasion and influence are key.

Many sales books focus solely on techniques and tactics, reducing the process to a stereotype approach. This author takes a different viewpoints. He emphasizes the importance of understanding the human element at the heart of every sale. He goes into the psychology of buying and selling, exploring the emotional motivations, unspoken desires, and subtle nuances that guide customer decisions.

This book tells stories about successful salespeople who do things a bit differently. It also shares how some big companies use these ideas. The main point is that doing well in sales isn't about following a set pattern; it's about using your unique strengths and connecting with people in your own way.

This book isn't simply a collection of narratives. The author analyzes strategies of successful brands, gleaning insights into their winning strategies. He draws inspiration from the biographies of iconic figures, dissecting their communication tactics and understanding how they persuaded and inspired others. Additionally, he shares valuable lessons garnered from in-depth interviews with top performers across various industries, offering readers a diverse perspective on the art of selling.

This book goes beyond the narrow definition of "selling" and focus on the importance of relationship building. The author argues that true success doesn't come from pushing products but from building trust, understanding, and long-term connections with customers. He equips readers with the tools to become trusted advisors, valuable sources of information, and genuine partners in their clients' journeys.

Whether you're a seasoned salesperson looking to refine your approach, an entrepreneur seeking to grow your business, or someone simply interested in the art of influence and persuasion, "The Art of Selling" offers valuable insights for all. It's a book that challenges conventional wisdom, sparks reflection, and empowers you to discover your own unique path to success, regardless of your background or experience.

Finally, people don't remember the fancy packaging, they remember how you made them feel. This book is your guide to unlocking that power. Forget about hitting quotas and exceeding targets; it's about making a real difference, leaving a positive impact that resonates long after the transaction is done.

True success doesn't lie in fleeting sales figures; it lies in creating a positive impact and leaving a lasting impression and get a leverage in the market. This book is your roadmap to achieving that, not through manipulation or coercion, but through genuine connection, heartfelt service, and a commitment to making a difference.

This book holds the potential to not only transform your sales approach but also unlock your potential to influence, connect, and achieve in every facet of your life.

1. Profit Magic: Turning Pain Points to Profits

In today's competitive market, simply having a good product or service isn't enough. To truly stand out and capture customer attention, you need to sell by adding value. This approach shifts the focus from just pushing features to understanding and alleviating customers' pain points, proposing solutions that make their lives better.

Finding the Pain:

The first step in selling by adding value is identifying your target audience's pain points. These are the challenges, frustrations, or unmet needs they face in their daily lives. Conduct thorough market research, engage in customer interviews, and understand the genuine problems to discover these pain points.

Here are some questions to ask:

What challenges do your customers face?

What are their current solutions (and why are they unsatisfactory)?

What frustrations do they encounter?

What unmet needs do they have?

Turning Pain into Value:

Once you understand the pain points, you can tailor your approach to offer solutions that truly resonate. This involves crafting a value proposition that clearly articulates how your product or service addresses these specific needs.

Focus on:

Benefits over features: Don't just list features; explain how they translate into concrete benefits that solve the customer's problem.

Quantifiable results: Whenever possible, use data, statistics, or case studies to showcase the measurable improvements your product brings.

Emotional connection: Speak to the emotional impact of solving their pain points. How will their lives be easier, happier, or more productive?

Uniqueness: Why should they choose you over competitors? Highlight your unique selling proposition and address any potential concerns.

Putting it into practice:

Here's how selling by adding value can translate into specific actions:

For a software company: Instead of just focusing on technical features, emphasize how your software saves users time, reduces errors, and increases productivity, addressing their pain points around efficiency and workload.

For a financial advisor: Don't just offer investment products; focus on understanding clients' financial goals and anxieties, offering personalized solutions that address their concerns about security, retirement planning, or wealth management.

The Benefits of Adding Value:

Selling by adding value isn't just a feel-good philosophy; it's a proven strategy with tangible benefits:

Increased customer satisfaction and loyalty: Customers who feel their needs are understood and addressed are more likely to become loyal advocates.

Stronger brand differentiation: By focusing on solutions, you stand out from competitors who simply sell features.

Higher closing rates: When customers understand the value you offer, they're more likely to say yes.

Improved customer lifetime value: Satisfied customers are more likely to repurchase and recommend your products to others.

Selling by adding value is a continuous process. Regularly revisit your market research, stay updated on customer needs, and refine your value proposition to maintain a competitive edge and build lasting customer relationships.

When you become a problem-solver rather than just a salesperson, you can unlock the true power of selling by adding value and achieve sustainable success in the marketplace.

2. Authentic Boost: Your Sales Journey

In a world saturated with marketing messages and curated online personas, authenticity has become a powerful differentiator for businesses. Customers today crave genuine connections, transparency, and brands that align with their values. This is where being authentic with customers becomes not just a feel-good practice, but a strategic imperative for driving sales and building lasting relationships. Many people think catchy words, tall and tricky claims without any real value will sale more. Yes, some customers get influenced but if when they do not find any real value, they go away and damage more in the long run.

Why Authenticity Matters:

Here are some key reasons why embracing authenticity drives sales:

Trust and Credibility: Consumers are inundated with marketing messages, constantly questioning their validity. Authenticity cuts through the noise, fostering trust and establishing your brand as reliable and trustworthy.

Emotional Connection: Authenticity allows customers to connect with your brand on a deeper level, beyond just product features. Sharing your brand story, values, and purpose resonates with their emotions, creating a loyal following.

Transparency and Honesty: Customers appreciate honesty and transparency, even if it means admitting imperfections or limitations. This builds trust and loyalty, encouraging customers to believe in your brand's commitment to their well-being.

Differentiation: In a crowded marketplace, authenticity helps you stand out from competitors. It allows you to showcase your unique personality and values, attracting customers who resonate with your brand identity.

Word-of-Mouth Marketing: Authentic interactions create positive word-of-mouth marketing. When customers feel respected and valued, they're more likely to share their positive experiences with others, driving organic growth.

Examples of Being Authentic with Customers:

Accept Imperfections: Don't shy away from showcasing the human side of your brand. Share candid stories, behind-the-scenes glimpses, and even acknowledge occasional mistakes. This relatable approach fosters trust and connection.

Value Customer Feedback: Actively seek and respond to customer feedback, both positive and negative. Show customers you care about their opinions and implement changes based on their insights. This demonstrates transparency and a commitment to improvement.

Personalize Interactions: Treat each customer as an individual, not just a transaction. You can note down their preferences, personalize offers, and engage in genuine conversations. This creates a sense of value and connection.

Empower Your Employees: Foster a culture of authenticity within your team. Empower employees to answer questions honestly, offer solutions even if they require extra effort, and connect with customers on a personal level.

Show Your Values: Stand for something bigger than just profit. Support causes you believe in, engage in social responsibility initiatives, and communicate your values authentically. This attracts customers who share your values and creates a strong brand identity.

Solutions for Implementing Authenticity:

Conduct Employee Training: Train your team on the importance of authenticity and equip them with the skills to engage in genuine interactions with customers.

Encourage Transparency: Foster a culture of open communication within your organization and encourage employees to be transparent with customers.

Utilize Feedback Mechanisms: Create effective channels for collecting and responding to customer feedback, showing them their voices are heard and valued.

Personalize Customer Interactions: Leverage technology and data to personalize communication and offers based on individual customer preferences.

Live Your Values: Ensure your internal practices and policies align with your publicly stated values. Authentic actions speak louder than words.

Find your authentic voice: What makes your brand unique? What stories can you tell? Don't copy trends; discover your own authentic style.

Be vulnerable: Sharing challenges and setbacks can humanize your brand and foster trust.

Focus on value, not just sales: Focus on providing true value to your customers, and sales will naturally follow.

Stay consistent: Authenticity needs to be reflected in all aspects of your brand, from marketing to customer service.

Be patient: Building trust and loyalty takes time. Stay committed to your authentic approach and the results will come.

Authenticity is not a one-time effort; it's a continuous journey. By consistently striving to be genuine, transparent, and value-driven in your interactions with customers, you build trust, foster loyalty, and ultimately drive sustainable sales growth. So, be yourself, be honest, and watch your brand flourish in the age of authenticity.

3. EmoSelling: The Emotional Sales Ride

Selling is inherently emotional, impacting both the seller and the buyer on a deeper level than just exchanging goods or services for money. Here are some examples to illustrate:

From the Buyer's Perspective:

- **Fear of Missing Out (FOMO):** Limited-time offers, exclusive products, or social proof ("everyone else is buying it!") can trigger FOMO, driving impulsive purchases based on emotions rather than pure need.
- **Aspiration and Identity:** We often buy things that project the image we want to portray or the person we aspire to be. A luxury watch might represent success, while a fitness tracker reflects a desire for health and wellness.
- **Nostalgia and Connection:** Products can evoke memories or emotional connections, influencing buying decisions. A

childhood toy re-released can trigger joyful memories, while a gift personalized with sentimental value sparks deeper meaning.

- **Trust and Empathy:** Feeling understood and cared for by the seller builds trust and rapport, making customers more open to buying. A salesperson who listens to concerns and offers genuine solutions creates a positive emotional connection.

From the Seller's Perspective:

- **Passion and Belief:** Genuine enthusiasm for the product or service is contagious. Sellers who believe in what they're selling can convey that passion to customers, fostering trust and excitement.
- **Empathy and Emotional Intelligence:** Understanding the customer's emotions and adapting communication accordingly is crucial. Recognizing hesitation, excitement, or fear allows the seller to tailor their approach for a more positive outcome.

- **Handling Objections and Building Value:** Addressing concerns with emotional intelligence can mitigate resistance and build trust. Highlighting the emotional benefits of the product (peace of mind, joy, fulfillment) can further reinforce its value.
- **Celebration and Connection:** Celebrating a successful sale creates a positive emotional bond between seller and buyer, increasing customer loyalty and potential for future business.

Examples in Action:

- A car salesperson, sensing a customer's excitement about a family road trip, highlights the car's safety features and spacious interior, appealing to their emotional desire for a secure and memorable experience.
- A travel agent, noticing a couple's hesitation about a luxury vacation, shares stories of past clients who experienced joy and connection through similar trips, tapping into their aspirations for romance and adventure.

- A nonprofit fundraiser, aware of potential donors' fears and concerns about impact, showcases heartwarming stories of individuals helped by their organization, appealing to their sense of empathy and desire to make a difference.

Successful selling goes beyond just product features and prices. By understanding and engaging with the emotions of both yourself and your customers, you can create a more meaningful and impactful sales experience that leads to loyal customers and sustainable growth.

Although emotions play a significant role in influencing purchase decisions, but to say most selling is done primarily based on emotions requires some nuance. While emotions are undeniable drivers, a balanced perspective acknowledges other factors at play.

Here's a breakdown:

The Emotional Pull:

- **Desire and Aspiration:** We're drawn to products that evoke positive emotions, align with our self-image, or fulfill our desires for security, belonging, or status.
- **Fear and Urgency:** Limited-time offers, scarcity tactics, or highlighting potential negative consequences can trigger fear and prompt impulsive purchases.
- **Nostalgia and Connection:** Products that evoke positive memories or emotional connections hold sentimental value and influence buying decisions.
- **Social Proof and Validation:** Seeing others use a product or service builds trust and validates its appeal, influencing our choices.

Beyond Emotions:

- **Rational Justification:** After the initial emotional pull, we often seek **rational justification** for our purchases. We analyze

features, compare prices, and research benefits to confirm a sound decision.
- **Practical Needs and Problem-Solving:** Not all buying decisions are purely emotional. Sometimes, we genuinely need a product to solve a practical problem, improve our lives, or fulfill a specific function.
- **Ethical Considerations and Values:** Increasingly, consumers consider ethical sourcing, sustainability, and alignment with their personal values when making purchases.

A Balanced View:

While emotions undoubtedly play a crucial role, they are rarely the sole driver of purchase decisions. We are complex beings guided by a **mixture of emotions, logic, values, and practical needs**. The relative weight of each element varies depending on the product, situation, and individual consumer.

Think of it as a spectrum:

- **Impulsive buys:** Driven primarily by emotional triggers like FOMO or nostalgia.
- **Emotional connections:** Products evoke strong feelings and personal meaning, influencing the decision with some rational justification.
- **Informed choices:** Emotional pull exists, but thorough research, comparison, and value assessment take priority.
- **Functional purchases:** Based primarily on practical needs and problem-solving, with minimal emotional influence.

Understanding the full spectrum helps businesses create effective marketing and sales strategies. Appealing to emotions can attract attention and initial interest, but building trust and loyalty requires addressing practical needs, offering value, and aligning with consumers' values.

I hope this clarifies the role of emotions in selling and provides a more nuanced perspective on purchase decisions. Successful selling involves acknowledging the emotional connection but balancing it with other factors for true effectiveness.

Here are some examples of selling goods based on emotions:

Appealing to Desire and Aspiration:

- **Luxury brands:** They associate their products with success, exclusivity, and status, leveraging aspirations for a certain lifestyle.
- **Fitness trackers and athletic wear:** They play on desires for self-improvement, health, and a fit and active lifestyle.
- **Makeup and beauty products:** They tap into desires for attractiveness, confidence, and self-expression.

Triggering Fear and Urgency:

- **Limited-time sales and flash offers:** They create a sense of scarcity and FOMO (fear of missing out), encouraging impulsive purchases.
- **Seasonal promotions:** Holiday campaigns or back-to-school deals trigger the fear of not

being prepared or missing out on the "perfect" gift.
- **Products promising quick solutions:** Weight loss supplements, wrinkle creams, or hair restoration options play on fears of physical imperfections and the desire for instant results.

Evoking Nostalgia and Connection:

- **Classic toys or childhood products:** They rekindle happy memories and emotional connections to the past.
- **Personalized gifts:** Customized items with names, dates, or special messages create sentimental value and emotional attachment.
- **Local food and handcrafted products:** They tap into feelings of community, supporting local businesses, and preserving tradition.

Using Social Proof and Validation:

- **Celebrity endorsements and influencer marketing:** People trust and aspire to celebrities, so their recommendations hold weight.

- **Customer testimonials and social media reviews:** Seeing others enjoy a product builds trust and validates its appeal.
- **Products associated with popular trends or events:** People want to feel included and on-trend, influencing buying decisions.

While emotions play a significant role, **ethical considerations and practical needs** should also be addressed for sustainable success. A balanced approach that respects customers' values and offers genuine value propositions will build trust and loyalty in the long run.

4. Relationship Gold: Beyond Transactions

Gone are the days of the pushy salesperson, barking features and manipulating customers. Today's secret weapon is building genuine relationships. People buy from those they trust, understand, and value. It's not about closing deals; it's about creating connections that last far beyond the initial purchase.

Why Relationships Matter:

- Trust is the foundation: Customers are bombarded with marketing messages; they crave authenticity and sincerity. Building trust fosters open communication and fosters long-term partnerships.
- Understanding needs: It's not just about selling a product; it's about solving a customer's problem. By actively listening

and understanding their needs, you tailor solutions that resonate.

- Building value beyond the product: True value lies in exceeding expectations. Offer insights, support, and genuine care, creating a relationship that extends beyond the transaction.

Examples of Relationship-Based Selling:

- The Consultant, not the Closer: Imagine a financial advisor, not simply pushing products, but understanding a client's financial goals and crafting a personalized plan. This builds trust and positions them as a long-term partner.

- The Educator, not the Pitcher: A software salesperson, instead of bombarding features, takes the time to understand the company's workflow and demonstrates how their product solves specific pain points. This adds value and fosters trust.

- The Community Builder: A real estate agent throws neighborhood events, connecting potential buyers with the community and demonstrating their genuine interest in their well-being, not just a quick sale.

Solutions for Building Relationships:

- Active Listening: Focus on understanding, not just waiting to speak. Ask open-ended questions and truly listen to their responses.
- Empathy & Understanding: Put yourself in their shoes. What are their challenges, goals, and concerns? Tailor your approach accordingly.
- Genuine Communication: Be honest, transparent, and avoid sales jargon. Speak like a human, not a script.
- Value-Added Content: Share industry insights, offer free consultations, or provide helpful resources. Be a trusted advisor, not just a salesperson.
- Follow-up & Support: Don't disappear after the sale. Check in regularly, offer

support, and be there to answer questions.

Remember:

- Relationships take time and effort: Don't expect instant results. Be patient, nurture the connection, and provide consistent value.
- It's a two-way street: Genuinely care about your customer's success. Their wins are your wins.
- Focus on quality, not quantity: Prioritize building meaningful connections over chasing quick sales.

By this relationship approach, you transform from a salesperson into a trusted advisor, building not just sales, but loyal customers and long-term partnerships.

5. Service Superhero: Exceptional Customer moments

In the fiercely competitive FMCG landscape, where brand loyalty is fickle and choices abound, exceptional customer service emerges as a powerful differentiator. Going beyond the expected and exceeding customer expectations isn't just a feel-good practice; it's a strategic investment that fuels brand advocacy, builds loyalty, and ultimately drives sales.

The Power of "Extra Mile" Service:

Exceptional customer service isn't simply about resolving complaints efficiently. It's about proactively creating positive experiences that resonate with customers on an emotional level. This translates to:

Increased brand loyalty: Customers who feel valued and appreciated are more likely to repurchase from the brand and become loyal advocates.

Positive word-of-mouth: Exceptional experiences get shared, driving organic marketing and attracting new customers.

Enhanced brand image: Positive customer experiences contribute to a strong brand reputation, instilling trust and confidence.

Improved customer lifetime value: Loyal customers spend more over time, contributing to sustainable growth.

Reduced customer churn: Satisfied customers are less likely to switch to competitors.

FMCG Giants Leading the Way:

Several Indian FMCG brands have mastered the art of exceeding customer expectations:

ITC: Known for its "Caring & Sharing" philosophy, ITC goes beyond product quality with initiatives like Project Sunehra, supporting farmers, and its 'Welcome ITC' program, offering personalized travel assistance.

Godrej Consumer Products: Recognizing the importance of after-sales service, Godrej offers prompt and efficient service calls, exceeding customer expectations in resolving product issues.

Marico: Marico's "Parachute Kalpavriksha" initiative empowers rural women with skill development and microloans, creating value beyond the product and fostering genuine connections.

Nestle: Committed to sustainability and social responsibility, Nestle's initiatives like Project Nanhi Kali and its focus on water conservation resonate with conscious consumers, driving brand preference.

Guiding Principles for FMCG Success:

Here are some actionable steps FMCG brands can take to implement exceptional customer service:

Emphasize Personalization: Move beyond generic interactions. Utilize data insights to understand individual customer needs and preferences, offering personalized recommendations and service experiences.

Adopt Proactive Communication: Don't wait for complaints. Proactively reach out to customers with updates, product information, and loyalty programs, demonstrating genuine care and engagement.

Empower Employees: Equip frontline staff with the training and resources to handle customer inquiries promptly and effectively, going the extra mile to resolve issues and exceed expectations.

Leverage Technology: Utilize technology to facilitate seamless customer interactions. Implement chatbots, self-service portals, and omnichannel communication channels to provide convenient and efficient support.

Create Memorable Experiences: Surprise and delight customers with unexpected gestures. Offer loyalty rewards, personalized coupons, or exclusive product samples, creating moments that go beyond the ordinary transaction.

Measure and Adapt: Regularly track customer feedback and satisfaction metrics. Use data to identify areas for improvement and continuously adapt your service strategies to ensure consistency and exceed expectations.

Focus on Building Relationships: Customer service is about building lasting relationships. Foster genuine connections with customers through personalized interactions, social media engagement, and community initiatives.

Empower Social Responsibility: Align your service practices with your brand's values and social responsibility initiatives. Consumers increasingly connect with brands that demonstrate genuine care for people and the planet.

Adopt Continuous Learning: Customer expectations are constantly evolving. Encourage a culture of continuous learning within your organization, ensuring employees are equipped to adapt and deliver exceptional service in an ever-changing landscape.

Excelling in customer service is a journey, not a destination. Implementing these strategies and nurturing a culture of service excellence will enable your FMCG brand to create loyal customers, drive sales, and stand out in the competitive market. By truly going the extra mile, you invest not just in customer satisfaction, but in the sustainable growth and success of your brand.

6. Brand Charisma: Company First, Product Second

The statement "First People buy the Company or Brand, then buy the Product" holds some truth, but requires a nuanced understanding. While brand loyalty and company values can certainly influence purchasing decisions, it's not always about buying the company first and then the product.

Here's a breakdown of the different perspectives:

Supporting the Argument:

- **Brand Loyalty:** People who identify with a brand's values, mission, or story are more likely to trust and support them, buying their products even if there are similar alternatives available.
- **Emotional Connection:** Brands that build positive emotional connections with consumers through storytelling, humor, or

social responsibility can create a loyal following who choose their products based on that connection.

- **Reputation and Trust:** Companies with a strong reputation for quality, ethics, and sustainability can attract customers who prioritize those values even if the product itself isn't the cheapest or most readily available.

Nuances and Counter examples:

- **Product-Driven Purchases:** Many purchases are based primarily on **practical needs, features, and value**. Consumers might compare product functionalities, prices, and performance across different brands, choosing the one that best meets their needs regardless of brand loyalty.
- **New Brands & Impulse Buys:** New brands with innovative products or attractive offers can attract customers even if they haven't established a strong brand identity yet.

- **Price Sensitivity:** In budget-conscious situations, price and value often outweigh brand loyalty, especially for everyday items.

A More Balanced View:

Instead of a strict hierarchy, consider it a **two-way relationship**:

- **Strong brands attract customers who align with their values and trust their offerings.**
- **Successful products build positive brand perceptions and customer loyalty.**

Here are some additional factors to consider:

- **Target audience:** Different demographics prioritize different factors when making purchases. Younger generations might be more swayed by brand image and social responsibility, while older generations might focus on practicality and value.
- **Product category:** Luxury goods often rely more on brand association and emotional

connection, while everyday items might be more heavily influenced by features and price.
- **Competitive landscape:** In saturated markets, strong brand identity can be a differentiator, while in less competitive markets, product quality and price might carry more weight.

Ultimately, **the decision to buy a product or support a brand is complex and influenced by various factors**. While brand loyalty and company values can play a significant role, especially for repeat purchases, understanding the full context and individual needs is crucial for accurate conclusions.

7. ShopJoy: Crafting a Playful Buying Adventure

In today's competitive marketplace, capturing and retaining customers requires constant innovation. Gamification emerges as a powerful tool, transforming the traditional buying process into an engaging and interactive experience. By tapping into the inherent human desire for fun, competition, and rewards, businesses can attract, engage, and ultimately convert more customers.

Understanding Gamification:

Gamification involves incorporating game-like elements, such as points, badges, leaderboards, challenges, and rewards, into non-game contexts. In the context of the buying process, this might involve:

Earning points for purchases or completing tasks.

Unlocking exclusive offers or discounts through challenges.

Competing for top positions on leaderboards and winning prizes.

Collecting virtual badges for achieving milestones.

Benefits of Gamified Buying:

Increased Engagement: Interactive elements pique interest and keep customers coming back for more.

Enhanced Brand Loyalty: Rewards and recognition develop positive associations with the brand.

Improved Customer Acquisition: Gamification drives word-of-mouth marketing and attracts new customers.

Valuable Customer Data: Insights from game interactions inform targeted marketing and product development.

Personalized Customer Experiences: Tailored challenges and rewards cater to individual preferences.

Examples of Gamification in Action:

Retail stores: Customers earn points for purchases, unlock discounts through scavenger hunts, and compete for the "top shopper" badge.

Subscription services: Users level up by completing tasks, earn badges for consistent engagement, and unlock exclusive content.

E-commerce platforms: Customers collect virtual trophies for referring friends, participate in flash sales with time-based challenges, and win bonus points for writing reviews.

Financial institutions: Users receive badges for reaching savings goals, compete in budgeting challenges, and earn rewards for learning financial skills.

Solutions for Implementing Gamification:

Clearly define your goals and target audience.

Choose appropriate game mechanics that align with your brand and objectives.

Integrate gamification seamlessly into your existing buying process.

Make sure the game is fun, fair, and easy to understand.

Offer meaningful rewards that incentivize desired behaviors.

Track and analyze user engagement to optimize your gamification strategy.

Successful gamification goes beyond simply adding points and badges. It's about creating a holistic experience that motivates, engages, and builds a lasting connection with your customers. So, unleash your creativity, explore the possibilities, and gamify your buying process to unlock a world of engagement and growth!

8. Buyer Bliss: Mastering The Art of Persuasion

While the statement "no one wants to be sold" might seem extreme, it reflects a fundamental shift in how consumers interact with brands and make purchasing decisions. Today's empowered buyers are bombarded with marketing messages, and traditional "hard sell" tactics often feel intrusive and inauthentic. So, how can businesses adapt their sales and marketing strategies to resonate with this new reality?

Understanding the Shift:

Information Power: Consumers have unprecedented access to information online, empowering them to research, compare, and make informed decisions independently. They don't need a salesperson to tell them everything about a product.

Value-Driven Decisions: Today's buyers prioritize value over mere features. They seek brands that align with their values, offer solutions to their problems, and provide a positive experience.

Transparency and Authenticity: Consumers crave genuine connections with brands. They see through inauthentic advertising and appreciate transparency in pricing, practices, and communication.

From Selling to Helping:

Focus on Value, Not Features: Highlight how your product/service improves the customer's life, solves their problems, or fulfills their needs. Don't just list features; tell stories that resonate.

Become a Trusted Advisor: Offer valuable information and resources, even if they don't directly lead to a sale. Build trust and establish yourself as an expert in your field.

Engage in Authentic Storytelling: Share your brand story, values, and the people behind the product. Connect with customers on an emotional level and build genuine relationships.

Empower, Don't Pressure: Provide clear information, transparent pricing, and easy-to-understand options. Let customers make informed decisions at their own pace.

Personalize the Experience: Tailor your communication and recommendations based on individual needs and preferences. Make the buyer feel valued and understood.

Examples:

Instead of: "This phone has the best camera on the market!" Try: "Capture life's precious moments with stunning clarity and vibrant colors. Our camera's AI technology ensures you never miss a perfect shot."

Instead of: "Sign up for our newsletter and get 10% off!" Try: "Get valuable tips and exclusive offers delivered straight to your inbox. We respect your privacy and won't spam you."

Instead of: "Our sales rep will contact you to discuss your needs." Try: "Explore our product guides and FAQs at your own pace. If you have questions, our friendly support team is just a click away."

It's not about abandoning sales entirely, but about shifting the focus from "selling" to "helping." By providing value, building trust, and empowering customers, brands can create a win-win situation where both parties thrive.

This is just a starting point, and the specific strategies you implement will depend on your industry, target audience, and brand identity. However, by embracing the "no one wants to be sold" mindset and focusing on building genuine connections with your customers, you can unlock a new era of success in today's dynamic market.

9. Partner Power: Unexpected Brand Alliance

In today's saturated market, brands constantly seek innovative ways to stand out and capture consumer attention. While traditional partnerships within the same industry or target audience have their merits, the real game-changers often lie in the realm of the unexpected. These seemingly incongruous collaborations, where brands from seemingly disparate universes come together, can spark curiosity, generate buzz, and ultimately drive sales by:

Reaching New Audiences: Partnering with a brand targeting a different demographic or with a distinct brand identity allows you to tap into an entirely new audience segment. This opens up unexplored sales potential and fosters brand awareness among previously unreachable consumers.

Boosting Brand Relevance: An unexpected partnership can inject novelty and excitement into your brand image, making it seem fresh and relevant in a rapidly evolving market. This can be particularly beneficial for mature brands seeking to revitalize their appeal.

Enhancing Brand Authenticity: When brands with strong, unique identities collaborate, it fosters a sense of authenticity and genuineness that resonates with consumers seeking genuine connections. This authenticity can translate into increased trust and brand loyalty.

Creating Unique Value Propositions: Unexpected partnerships often lead to innovative product collaborations or experiences that traditional partnerships wouldn't offer. This unique value proposition attracts consumers seeking differentiation and exclusivity, driving sales and excitement.

Amplifying Marketing Reach: By combining marketing resources and leveraging each other's social media followings, unexpected partnerships can significantly amplify marketing reach and brand exposure. This synergy can lead to exponential growth in brand awareness and customer acquisition.

Here are five successful examples of unexpected Global brand partnerships that demonstrate these benefits in action:

Supreme & The North Face: The streetwear giant Supreme collaborated with outdoor apparel brand The North Face, resulting in a highly sought-after collection of jackets, backpacks, and accessories. This unlikely pairing appealed to Supreme's fashion-conscious audience while introducing The North Face to a new, trendsetting demographic, boosting sales for both brands.

IKEA & LEGO: Furniture giant IKEA teamed up with toymaker LEGO to create a collection of playful and functional storage solutions. This partnership resonated with families seeking both design-conscious storage and engaging playtime experiences, leading to impressive sales and positive brand perception for both companies.

Netflix & Spotify: Streaming giants Netflix and Spotify partnered to offer a unique recommendation feature. Spotify suggested music based on what users were watching on Netflix, creating a seamless entertainment experience and driving engagement for both platforms.

KFC & Crocs: Fast food chain KFC collaborated with shoemaker Crocs to create limited-edition, fried chicken-scented Crocs. While seemingly bizarre, this partnership went viral, generating massive publicity and selling out instantly, demonstrating the power of unexpected humor and exclusivity.

Heinz & Heinz: Ketchup brand Heinz partnered with itself, launching a limited-edition "Mayonnaise on Everything" sauce aimed at mayonnaise enthusiasts. This self-aware and playful campaign generated significant buzz and sales, showing how even seemingly internal partnerships can be impactful.

These examples highlight the potential of unexpected brand partnerships to drive sales and engagement. However, it's crucial to ensure the partnership aligns with both brand identities and resonates with the target audience. Careful planning, creative execution, and a clear understanding of potential benefits are essential for maximizing the success of these unlikely liaisons.

In a world where consumers crave novelty and authenticity, brands that dare to think outside the box and forge unexpected partnerships can reap significant rewards, unlocking new markets, strengthening brand relevance, and ultimately driving sales success. So, be bold, be creative, and explore the unexpected – your next big partnership might just be waiting around the corner.

The Unexpected Advantage

In the hyper-competitive Indian market, brands are constantly seeking innovative ways to stand out and capture consumer attention. While traditional partnerships within similar industries hold value, partnering with unexpected brands can unlock a treasure trove of benefits, driving sales and brand awareness to new heights. These collaborations challenge preconceived notions, generate buzz, and tap into entirely new customer segments, leading to mutually beneficial growth. Let's delve into the power of unexpected brand partnerships and explore some successful examples in India:

Why Unexpected Partnerships Work

- **Novelty and Excitement:** Consumers crave surprises and experiences that break the mold. Unexpected partnerships pique their curiosity, generate buzz, and foster deeper engagement.
- **Reaching New Audiences:** By joining forces with a brand from a seemingly unrelated industry, you gain access to their established customer base, expanding your reach and tapping into new demographics.
- **Enhanced Brand Image:** Stepping outside your comfort zone demonstrates innovation, boldness, and a willingness to

experiment, making your brand appear more dynamic and relevant.

- **Synergy and Value Creation:** Combining strengths and resources from different industries can lead to innovative products, services, or marketing campaigns that resonate with consumers on a deeper level.
- **Cost-Effective Marketing:** Collaborations can leverage each other's strengths and resources, optimizing marketing budgets and amplifying reach without significant individual investments.

5 Successful Unexpected Brand Partnerships in India:

Zomato & Bumble: In 2020, food delivery platform Zomato collaborated with dating app Bumble for a Valentine's Day campaign titled "Eat. Date. Repeat." The campaign offered Bumble users exclusive discounts on Zomato orders, encouraging them to order food for dates or post-date cravings. This unexpected pairing resonated with young singles, boosting both brands' visibility and engagement.

Netflix & Myntra: In 2021, streaming giant Netflix partnered with fashion e-commerce platform Myntra to launch a limited-edition clothing line inspired by popular Netflix shows like "Money Heist" and "Stranger Things." This collaboration allowed fans to express their fandom through fashion, leading to a surge in online sales and brand loyalty for both entities.

Spotify & Domino's: In 2022, music streaming platform Spotify teamed up with pizza chain Domino's for a unique campaign. Spotify curated personalized playlists based on customers' pizza orders, creating a fun and engaging way to enhance the dining experience. This partnership leveraged the emotional connection music has with food, driving repeat business and brand recall for both companies.

Flipkart & Marvel: In 2019, e-commerce giant Flipkart collaborated with Marvel to launch a co-branded loyalty program. The program offered exclusive merchandise, early access to sales, and other benefits to Marvel fans, attracting a new customer segment to Flipkart and strengthening brand affinity among existing Marvel enthusiasts.

Uber & Dunzo: In 2020, ride-hailing app Uber partnered with hyperlocal delivery platform Dunzo to offer grocery deliveries to Uber users. This strategic alliance addressed the growing demand for quick and convenient grocery delivery while expanding Dunzo's customer base and increasing Uber's service offerings.

Key Considerations for Successful Unexpected Partnerships:

- Shared Values and Target Audience: Ensure the partner brand aligns with your core values and targets a similar or complementary customer segment.
- Clear Objectives and Benefits: Define clear goals for the partnership and ensure both parties benefit from the collaboration.

- Creative Activation and Communication: Develop a unique and engaging campaign that captures the essence of the partnership and resonates with the target audience.
- Authenticity and Transparency: Maintain transparency and authenticity throughout the collaboration to build trust and credibility with consumers.

The Indian market is ripe for brands to accept the power of unexpected partnerships. By thinking outside the box and forging collaborations with seemingly unrelated brands, companies can unlock new marketing avenues, expand their reach, and drive sales in innovative ways. As consumer expectations evolve and the demand for novelty increases, these strategic alliances will continue to play a pivotal role in shaping the future of brand success in India. So, dare to challenge convention, explore the possibilities.

10. PersonaCraft: Tailoring Sales with Precision

In today's digital age, where consumers are bombarded with marketing messages from every corner, standing out from the crowd requires more than just competitive pricing or flashy advertisements. The key to capturing hearts and wallets lies in creating a personalized touch, a genuine connection that resonates with individual needs and values. This personalized approach isn't just a feel-good strategy; it's a proven method for driving sales and fostering long-term customer loyalty.

Why Personalization Matters:

Cuts Through the Noise: In a world saturated with marketing messages, personalization helps businesses stand out by speaking directly to individual consumers, addressing their specific needs and interests. This targeted approach cuts through the noise, grabbing attention and leaving a lasting impression.

Builds Trust and Credibility: When customers feel seen and understood, they're more likely to trust the brand and believe in its offerings. Personalized interactions showcase genuine care and attention, fostering a sense of authenticity that resonates deeply with consumers.

Boosts Brand Loyalty: Personalized experiences strengthen the emotional connection between brands and customers. Feeling valued and appreciated encourages repeat purchases, positive word-of-mouth referrals, and brand advocacy.

Drives Engagement and Conversion: Personalized marketing messages, product recommendations, and offers are more likely to capture attention and prompt action. Customers are more receptive to information that directly addresses their needs and preferences, leading to higher conversion rates and increased sales.

How Big Brands in India are Embracing Personalization:

Here are few examples of how leading Indian brands are incorporating personalization into their strategies:

Myntra: This fashion e-commerce platform leverages user data to curate personalized product recommendations and outfit suggestions. Myntra's "Style Match" feature analyzes past purchases and browsing behavior to predict future preferences, offering recommendations tailored to individual styles.

Solution: Utilize customer data to create personalized shopping experiences across platforms. Offer virtual stylists based on preferences, and recommend outfits for specific occasions or trends.

Zomato: This food delivery giant personalizes the user experience by recommending restaurants based on past orders, location, and dietary preferences. Additionally, Zomato's "Foodie Score" gamifies the user experience, rewarding loyal customers with personalized offers and discounts.

Solution: Implement recommendation algorithms for restaurants and dishes based on individual preferences and dietary restrictions. Offer loyalty programs with personalized rewards and early access to new features.

HDFC Bank: This leading bank personalizes financial products and services through its "Go Digital" initiative. By analyzing customer data, HDFC recommends relevant investment options, credit cards, and other financial products tailored to individual needs and goals.

Solution: Offer AI-powered financial advisors who suggest personalized investment plans and wealth management strategies based on individual profiles and risk tolerance.

Flipkart: This e-commerce giant personalizes its customer journey through targeted communication and dynamic pricing. Flipkart analyzes purchase history and browsing behavior to send customers personalized emails and notifications about relevant products and deals.

Solution: Offer targeted discounts and promotions based on past purchases and wishlists. Send personalized notifications about price drops or restocks on desired items.

MakeMyTrip: This travel booking platform personalizes travel recommendations based on past trips, interests, and budget. MakeMyTrip's "MyTrips" feature suggests destinations and experiences tailored to individual preferences, making travel planning easier and more enjoyable.

Solution: Offer curated travel packages based on user profiles and past travel patterns. Recommend hidden gems and local experiences alongside tourist destinations.

Personalized Strategy:

While these examples showcase successful implementations, personalization isn't a one-size-fits-all approach. Here are key elements to consider when crafting your personalized strategy:

Data Collection and Analysis: Leverage customer data (with consent) to understand individual preferences, purchase history, and online behavior.

Segmentation and Targeting: Segment your audience based on relevant demographics, interests, and needs to deliver targeted messaging and offers.

Omnichannel Experience: Ensure consistent personalization across all touchpoints, from websites and apps to social media and email marketing.

Dynamic Content and Offers: Create dynamic content and offers that adapt to individual preferences and browsing behavior in real-time.

Customer Feedback and Iterations: Continuously gather and analyze customer feedback to refine your personalization strategy and ensure it remains relevant.

Personalization is not just a trend; it's the future of customer engagement and sales success. By prioritizing genuine connections and catering to individual needs, brands can unlock a higher level of customer loyalty and brand advocacy. Personalization is about building relationships, not just transactions. Adopt this approach, and watch your brand thrive in the age of empowered and discerning consumers.

11. Quality Quest: The Key to Longevity

"Quality is the key" - a powerful statement, yet its true meaning and actionable solutions often remain elusive. While everyone desires quality, achieving and maintaining it requires constant analysis, improvement, and adaptability. Here common pain points that hinder its attainment are identified, and proposed solutions to unlock its full potential.

Understanding Quality: A Multifaceted Gem

Quality isn't a singular concept; it's a multifaceted gem with different facets depending on the context. In business, it's often defined as "conformance to requirements and fitness for use." This implies that a product or service meets specified standards and delivers value to its intended purpose. However, quality should also encompass elements like customer satisfaction, innovation, and sustainability.

Pain Points on the Quality Journey

The path to achieving quality is paved with roadblocks and challenges. Here are some common pain points:

- Lack of Clear Definition: What constitutes "quality" can be subjective and vary across stakeholders. Without a clear, shared definition, efforts become scattered and misaligned.
- Short-Term Focus: Prioritizing profit margins or quick wins can lead to compromising quality for cost-cutting measures, ultimately harming long-term value.
- Siloed Thinking: Departmental boundaries or internal competition can create blind spots, hindering collaborative quality improvement efforts.
- Inadequate Measurement: Without reliable metrics and data, it's difficult to assess current quality, track progress, and identify areas needing improvement.

- Resistance to Change: Fear of disruption or lack of buy-in from employees can impede implementing necessary quality initiatives.
- Neglecting Customer Voice: Failing to gather and act upon customer feedback creates a disconnect between what's delivered and what's truly valued.
- Lack of Innovation: Sticking to outdated methods can make quality stagnant, failing to adapt to evolving needs and expectations.
- Unsustainable Practices: Compromising environmental or ethical standards for short-term gains eventually erodes trust and damages long-term brand reputation.

Solutions: Cultivating a Culture of Quality

Addressing these pain points requires a strategic and comprehensive approach. Here are solutions to consider:

- Define Quality Collectively: Involve all stakeholders (employees, customers, suppliers) in defining quality standards specific to your context and vision.

- Focus on Long-Term Value: Shift the mindset from short-term gains to sustainable value creation through investing in quality processes and employee development.
- Break Down Silos: Foster collaboration across departments, encouraging information sharing and alignment towards shared quality goals.
- Implement Robust Metrics: Develop measurable quality indicators across different aspects (e.g., product, service, employee satisfaction) and regularly track progress.
- Adopt Change Management: Create a culture of continuous improvement where change is seen as an opportunity for growth, supported by effective communication and training.
- Listen to Your Customers: Regularly gather and analyze customer feedback, using it to inform product development, service delivery, and quality improvement initiatives.
- Foster Innovation: Encourage a culture of experimentation and continuous improvement

to adapt to changing needs and maintain a competitive edge in quality.
- Integrate Sustainability: Embed ethical and environmental considerations into quality standards, ensuring long-term viability and building trust with stakeholders.

By identifying pain points, implementing solutions, and fostering a culture of continuous improvement, you can unlock the true potential of quality, leading to higher customer satisfaction, employee engagement, and sustainable success.

- Industry Specificity: While the pain points and solutions discussed apply broadly, tailoring them to your specific industry can enhance their effectiveness.
- Leadership Commitment: Demonstrated commitment from leadership is crucial for driving a quality culture and ensuring resources are allocated for improvement initiatives.
- Technology and Automation: Leveraging technology and automation can streamline quality processes, enhance data collection and

analysis, and free up resources for higher-level strategic thinking.
- Celebrating Success: Recognizing and celebrating quality achievements motivates employees and reinforces the importance of quality within the organization.
- External Benchmarking: Comparing your quality practices to industry leaders can provide valuable insights and identify areas for improvement.

Cultivating a quality culture is an ongoing process that requires dedication, collaboration, and adaptability. By embracing the journey and continually seeking improvement, you can unlock the true power of "quality is the key" and achieve sustainable success.

12. Resistance Vanish: Making Sales Smooth

"Removal of Resistance" in selling refers to addressing and overcoming objections a potential customer might have towards making a purchase. It's not about forcefully manipulating them, but rather understanding their concerns and presenting information that helps them feel comfortable moving forward.

Here are some key steps to effectively address resistance:

1. Actively listen and identify the resistance: Don't interrupt or dismiss objections. Listen carefully to understand the source of their hesitance. Is it the price, features, quality, brand trust, or something else?

2. Acknowledge and validate their concerns: Show them you understand their perspective and empathize with their worries. Don't downplay their objections or argue against them.

3. Ask clarifying questions: Gently probe deeper to fully understand the specific details behind their resistance. This helps tailor your response more effectively.

4. Address the objection directly: Provide clear, concise, and truthful information that directly addresses their concerns. Use data, testimonials, or product demonstrations to showcase value and build trust.

5. Highlight benefits and solutions: Frame your response by focusing on how your product or service solves their specific problem or fulfills their needs.

6. Offer options and compromises: If appropriate, provide alternative solutions or pricing options that could address their concerns without compromising your value proposition.

7. Focus on building trust and relationships: Let your genuine enthusiasm and knowledge shine through. Be transparent, patient, and respectful throughout the conversation.

8. Don't pressure or force a sale: If they're still hesitant, don't be pushy. Respect their decision and offer resources for further information or future consideration.

"Removal of Resistance" is an ongoing process. It's not always about closing the deal immediately. Sometimes, it's about building trust and laying the groundwork for future sales. By patiently addressing their concerns and demonstrating your value, you can ultimately lead them towards a confident and informed decision.

Here are some additional tips:

- Anticipate potential objections: Prepare responses beforehand for common concerns raised by customers in your industry.
- Practice your communication skills: Hone your active listening, empathy, and persuasion techniques to effectively address resistance.
- Monitor your body language: Maintain positive, open body language that projects confidence and trustworthiness.

- Continuously learn and adapt: Analyze your interactions and identify areas for improvement in your approach to overcoming resistance.

These strategies will help you to transform "Removal of Resistance" from a hurdle to a valuable opportunity to build trust, educate customers, and ultimately achieve your sales goals.

Big Companies Removing Resistance: Real-World Examples

1. Apple: Simplifying Technology with Powerful Storytelling:

Apple is renowned for its ability to overcome the "resistance" of complex technology by presenting it in a simple, elegant, and user-friendly way. They achieve this through several strategies:

- **Storytelling:** Apple doesn't just sell features, they paint a picture of how their products will enhance your life. Think about their iconic "Think Different" campaign or the emotional journeys depicted in their product launch videos.

- **Focus on Benefits:** Apple avoids technical jargon and emphasizes the user experience, highlighting how their products make people's lives easier, more creative, or more connected.
- **Seamless Integration:** Their ecosystem of products and services work seamlessly together, removing friction and simplifying tasks. Imagine buying an iPhone and it instantly working with your Macbook without any configuration struggles.
- **Premium Image:** While not explicitly removing resistance, Apple's premium image assures customers of quality and reliability, reducing concerns about potential issues.

By focusing on user experience, emotional connection, and simplified technology, Apple effectively addresses the "resistance" often associated with adopting new technology.

2. IKEA: Democratizing Furniture with Convenience and Affordability:

IKEA faced the challenge of selling furniture, often perceived as expensive and requiring assembly expertise. They tackled this "resistance" through innovative strategies:

- **Flat-Pack Magic:** IKEA revolutionized furniture packaging with flat-pack designs, making them easier to transport and assemble, addressing space and physical limitations.
- **Clear Instructions & Visual Guides:** They provide clear, step-by-step instructions with visual aids, reducing assembly anxiety and empowering even DIY novices.
- **Self-Service Model:** Their self-service model allows customers to browse, choose, and pack their furniture, reducing perceived sales pressure and empowering independent decision-making.
- **Affordability:** By utilizing efficient production and distribution systems, IKEA offers high-

quality furniture at competitive prices, overcoming the affordability hurdle.

By focusing and implementing above all areas, IKEA successfully removes the "resistance" associated with furniture purchase and assembly, making it accessible to a wider audience.

3. Netflix: Tailoring Content and Eliminating Friction:

Netflix faced the "resistance" of traditional media consumption, with limitations like fixed schedules and channel-surfing fatigue. They addressed this through:

- **Subscription Model:** Moving from pay-per-view to a subscription model reduced perceived financial risk and encouraged exploration of diverse content.
- **Personalized Recommendations:** Netflix utilizes algorithms to suggest content based on individual viewing habits, creating a sense of curated discovery and reducing the overwhelming feeling of choice.

- **Seamless Streaming:** Their user-friendly interface and focus on smooth streaming eliminate technical friction, making content instantly accessible.
- **Content Variety:** Offering a wide range of diverse and original content caters to various tastes and preferences, eliminating the risk of not finding something engaging.

Here are some additional examples of how companies have overcome resistance:

4. TOMS: Bridging the Gap Between Fashion and Social Impact:

TOMS faced the challenge of selling shoes in a saturated market while also promoting social impact. They addressed this through:

- **One-for-One Model:** With every purchase, TOMS donates a pair of shoes to a child in need, giving customers a feel-good factor and overcoming the "selfishness" objection often associated with luxury goods.

- **Transparency and Storytelling:** They transparently communicate their impact, showcasing the lives they touch and creating an emotional connection with buyers.
- **Fashionable Designs:** They offer stylish and trendy footwear, ensuring their products compete on both social impact and aesthetic appeal.

By combining fashion with social impact, TOMS overcame resistance from consumers looking for both stylish products and a way to make a difference.

5. Dollar Shave Club: Disrupting the Industry with Convenience and Value:

Dollar Shave Club faced the challenge of disrupting the established razor industry, known for high prices and inconvenient purchase cycles. They tackled this through:

- **Subscription Model:** Offering a convenient subscription model with affordable blades delivered directly to customers'

doorsteps, eliminating the need for frequent store visits and high one-time purchases.
- **Humor and Transparency:** Their humorous marketing campaigns and transparent pricing strategy resonated with consumers seeking value and a more relaxed brand experience.
- **Quality Assurance:** Despite the low price, they maintained high-quality blades, addressing the "cheap quality" concern associated with budget-friendly options.

By focusing on convenience, humor, transparency, and value, Dollar Shave Club successfully disrupted the razor industry, removing resistance from consumers seeking a better shaving experience.

6. Tesla: Overcoming the "Electric Car" Resistance with Innovation and Experience:

Tesla faced the challenge of selling electric cars, often seen as having limited range, high cost, and inconvenient charging infrastructure. They addressed this through:

- **Focus on Performance and Range:** Tesla prioritized long range and powerful electric motors, overcoming concerns about range anxiety and performance compared to gasoline cars.
- **Supercharger Network:** Building their own charging infrastructure network addressed concerns about charging availability and convenience.
- **Luxury and Technology:** They combined cutting-edge technology with luxurious design, making electric cars not just practical but desirable.

By focusing on performance, range, charging infrastructure, luxury, and technology, Tesla successfully overcame the resistance associated with electric vehicles and became a leader in the industry.

These are just a few examples. The most effective methods of removing resistance will vary depending on your industry, target audience, and specific product or service. By understanding the potential objections and implementing thoughtful strategies, you too can create a more seamless and persuasive buying experience for your customers.

13. Believe & Sell: Your Personal Sales Magic

Success often boils down to one key thing: believing in yourself first. Before winning over clients or sealing deals, it's crucial to have confidence in your own worth and abilities. This simple idea unlocks numerous advantages, making you a more convincing and genuine salesperson. Picture yourself approaching a potential client with confidence and certainty. It's not an act; it's a natural result of first convincing yourself of your expertise and the value you offer.

If you can sell a product or genuinely believe in its value, it means you genuinely like the product. When you genuinely like a product, it becomes easier to persuade customers. In many cases, salespeople struggle to convince customers because they aren't genuinely convinced about the product they're selling.

Why is selling to yourself crucial?

Boosts Confidence: Believing in yourself translates to exuding confidence – an essential ingredient for winning trust and overcoming objections. When you doubt your abilities, it shows, impacting your persuasiveness and credibility.

Enhances Authenticity: When you truly believe in your product or service, your passion shines through. This genuine enthusiasm resonates with clients, strengthening connections and establishing rapport.

Improves Communication: Conviction fosters clarity and articulation. You naturally communicate the value proposition effectively when you genuinely believe in it.

Increases Resilience: Selling is a challenging journey. Rejection and setbacks are inevitable. But selling to yourself first equips you with mental fortitude to bounce back and persevere.

So, how do you "sell" yourself first?

1. Know Your Strengths: Deep dive into your skills, knowledge, and experiences. Identify what makes

you unique and valuable. Write down your accomplishments and positive client testimonials.

2. Adopt Positive Self-Talk: Replace negative self-doubt with encouraging affirmations. Remind yourself of your past successes and visualize future achievements.

3. Practice Role-Playing: Rehearse presentations, pitches, and objections with a trusted friend or colleague. This hones your communication skills and boosts your confidence.

4. Seek Inspiration: Read biographies of successful salespeople, watch motivational videos, or surround yourself with positive and supportive individuals.

5. Celebrate Victories: Acknowledge and reward yourself for even minor wins. This reinforces positive self-belief and motivates you to keep pushing forward.

Selling to yourself isn't about arrogance; it's about building genuine self-belief and recognizing your unique value. By investing in yourself first, you unlock the potential to become a confident, persuasive, and ultimately, successful salesperson.

Adopt the journey of selling to yourself, and watch your sales career flourish!

14. Exquisite Service: Where Excellence Reigns

In today's saturated marketplace, where products increasingly resemble each other, the true differentiator lies not in what you sell, but in how you sell it. Service has transcended its traditional role as a post-purchase element; it is now the cornerstone of successful sales, unlocking customer loyalty, repeat business, and ultimately, sustained growth. This isn't just a theoretical concept; it's a data-driven imperative. Studies show that 73% of customers cite customer service as an important factor in their purchasing decisions, and a staggering 86% are willing to pay more for excellent service. So, how do we translate this knowledge into action? Let's delve into the concept of "Service is the Key to Sale," exploring the pain areas that hinder its implementation and offering practical solutions to transform your sales strategy.

Understanding the Pain Points:

Before building solutions, we must identify the roadblocks. Here are some common pain points that prevent many businesses from truly embracing service-centric sales:

Product-Centric Mindset: Traditional sales training often prioritizes product features and benefits over understanding customer needs. Salespeople might be incentivized to close deals quickly, neglecting the long-term relationship building aspect.

Lack of Customer Empathy: Sales teams may not fully understand the customer's challenges, resulting in irrelevant pitches and missed opportunities to provide value.

Disjointed Customer Journey: Inconsistent experiences across touchpoints - online, in-store, or over the phone - create confusion and dissatisfaction.

Inadequate Training and Empowerment: Salespeople might lack the skills and resources needed to effectively deliver exceptional service. This includes active listening, communication, and product knowledge beyond specifications.

Metrics Misalignment: Traditional sales metrics like conversion rates focus solely on closing deals, neglecting the long-term value of customer relationships.

Shifting the Paradigm: Solutions for Service-Centric Sales:

Empathy-Driven Approach: Train your sales team to actively listen and understand customer needs, challenges, and motivations. Encourage open-ended questions and focus on building rapport.

Value-Based Selling: Go beyond product features and highlight how your offering solves specific customer problems. Showcase tangible benefits and quantify the value proposition.

Omnichannel Consistency: Ensure seamless transitions across all customer touchpoints - online, offline, and through support channels. Offer consistent information, personalized communication, and a unified brand experience.

Skills Development: Equip your sales team with the tools and training they need to excel in service-centric selling. This includes communication skills, conflict resolution, negotiation strategies, and product knowledge beyond just specifications.

Relationship-Focused Metrics: Track and reward metrics that reflect the quality of customer interactions, such as customer satisfaction scores, Net Promoter Score (NPS), and customer lifetime value (CLTV).

The Power of Transformation:

By addressing these pain points and implementing service-centric solutions, businesses can unlock a multitude of benefits:

Increased Customer Satisfaction and Loyalty: Satisfied customers are more likely to return, recommend your brand, and advocate for your offerings.

Enhanced Brand Reputation: Exceptional service fosters positive word-of-mouth and builds brand trust, attracting new customers and differentiating you from competitors.

Improved Sales Performance: Building long-term relationships leads to repeat business and referrals, ultimately boosting sales and revenue.

Streamlined Sales Process: By understanding customer needs upfront, sales cycles become more efficient, reducing unnecessary objections and negotiations.

Reduced Customer Acquisition Costs: Loyal customers are cheaper to retain than acquire, contributing to cost savings and improved profitability.

Putting Theory into Practice:

Here are some actionable steps you can take to implement service-centric sales:

Conduct Customer Journey Mapping: Understand the touchpoints your customers experience and identify areas for improvement.

Empower Your Sales Team: Provide ongoing training and development opportunities to hone their service skills.

Implement Feedback Mechanisms: Gather customer feedback through surveys, reviews, and direct interactions to understand their needs and pain points.

Celebrate Service Excellence: Recognize and reward sales representatives who consistently deliver exceptional service.

Invest in Technology: Utilize customer relationship management (CRM) tools and other technologies to personalize interactions and track customer data effectively.

In a world where customers are bombarded with choices, exceptional service is no longer a luxury; it's a necessity for survival and growth. By adopting a service-centric approach, businesses can unlock a powerful competitive advantage, fostering lasting customer relationships, driving repeat business, and achieving sustainable success. Service is not just a department; it's a philosophy. Accept it, empower your team, and unlock the true potential of your sales strategy. By prioritizing service, you'll not only close deals, but you'll build something far more.

15. SellTales: Crafting Stories for Impact

In today's crowded marketplace, where attention spans are fleeting and competition is fierce, storytelling remains an enduring tool for brands to connect with their audience on an emotional level and ultimately drive sales. By weaving narratives that resonate, brands can bypass the noise and forge meaningful connections with consumers, fostering trust, loyalty, and ultimately, a purchase decision.

Why Stories Sell:

Stories tap into the fundamental human desire to connect, to be entertained, and to learn. They trigger emotional responses, creating a sense of empathy and understanding that drives engagement and memorability. Unlike dry facts and figures, stories paint vivid pictures in the mind, allowing consumers to experience the brand on a deeper level.

Benefits of Storytelling in Sales:

Increased Engagement: Stories capture attention and hold it longer than traditional marketing messages. They create an immersive experience that draws consumers in and makes them invested in the outcome.

Emotional Connection: By tapping into emotions, stories create a more powerful and lasting impression than rational appeals alone. When consumers connect with a brand on an emotional level, they are more likely to trust it and recommend it to others.

Enhanced Brand Recall: Stories are more memorable than facts. People remember stories long after they've forgotten a tagline or a statistic. This increased recall translates to better brand recognition and awareness.

Humanized Branding: Stories allow brands to showcase their values, personality, and mission in a relatable way. This helps to create a more humanized brand image, which is essential for building trust and loyalty.

Persuasive Power: Stories can subtly guide consumers towards a desired action, such as making a purchase or subscribing to a service. This is because stories resonate with emotions, not just logic, making them more persuasive than traditional sales pitches.

Indian Brands that Tell Stories Well:

Zomato: Zomato's "Feeding Millions of Stories" campaign showcased heartwarming stories of delivery partners and restaurant owners, highlighting the human connection made possible through their platform.

Lifebuoy: Lifebuoy's "#HogaSaafIndia" campaign used powerful storytelling to raise awareness about hygiene and sanitation, urging viewers to take action.

Tanishq: Tanishq's "Mia" campaign celebrated the bond between a mother and daughter, using storytelling to connect with their target audience on an emotional level.

BYJU'S: BYJU'S uses animation and engaging narratives to make learning fun and relatable for children, effectively differentiating themselves in the education sector.

Crafting Your Storytelling Strategy:

Know Your Audience: Who are you trying to reach? What are their needs, desires, and pain points? Understanding your audience is crucial for crafting stories that resonate with them.

Define Your Brand Story: What is your brand's purpose? What values do you stand for? What story do you want to tell the world? A clear brand story forms the foundation for all your storytelling efforts.

Find the Right Format: Choose the format that best suits your story and audience. This could be video, animation, blog posts, social media content, or even traditional advertising.

Focus on Emotion: Evoke emotions through your storytelling. Humor, nostalgia, surprise, and hope are all powerful tools for connecting with your audience.

Make it Authentic: Your story should be true to your brand's voice and identity. Consumers can spot inauthenticity a mile away, so be genuine and transparent.

Call to Action: Don't leave your audience hanging. Tell them what you want them to do next, whether it's visiting your website, making a purchase, or sharing your story.

Measure and Adapt: Track the results of your storytelling efforts and adapt your strategies based on what works and what doesn't.

Storytelling is not a one-time event; it's an ongoing journey. By consistently crafting and sharing stories that resonate with your audience, you can build deeper connections, drive sales, and create a brand that truly stands out in the marketplace.

Beyond these initial points, there are many other aspects to consider in crafting a successful storytelling strategy. Here are some additional resources you may find helpful:

Books: "Made to Stick" by Chip and Dan Heath, "Storytelling for Sales" by Carmine Gallo

Articles: "The Science of Storytelling: Why Stories Make Us Buy" by Harvard Business Review, "How to Use Storytelling to Sell Anything" by Forbes

Online Courses: "The Art of Storytelling for Social Media" by Udemy, "Storytelling for Brand Marketing" by LinkedIn Learning

16. Surprise Delight: Winning Customer Hearts

In the hyper-competitive world of business, where customer loyalty is fickle and attention spans are fleeting, surprise emerges as a powerful tool to not only stand out but also drive sales and build enduring relationships. By exceeding expectations and delivering unexpected value, brands can create moments of delight that resonate with customers, fostering trust and encouraging repeat business.

The Power of Surprise in Driving Sales

The element of surprise triggers positive emotions like joy, excitement, and gratitude, leaving a lasting impression on customers. This emotional connection translates to stronger brand recall, enhanced brand perception, and a willingness to recommend the brand to others. It can also boost sales by:

Increasing purchase value: Surprises can incentivize customers to upgrade their purchases, try new products, or spend more.

Encouraging repeat business: A positive surprise experience creates a strong association between the brand and positive emotions, motivating customers to return.

Triggering word-of-mouth marketing: When customers are genuinely surprised and delighted, they're more likely to share their experiences with friends and family, driving organic marketing.

Big Brands, Big Surprises:

Zomato: Their "Gold" subscription offers surprise rewards and cashback, keeping customers engaged and spending more.

Flipkart: They surprise customers with early access to sales, exclusive product launches, and personalized offers, creating a sense of exclusivity.

Netflix: They curate personalized recommendations and surprise viewers with hidden features and interactive content, enhancing engagement.

Airtel: They offer unexpected data boosts, free services, and personalized deals, exceeding customer expectations and fostering loyalty.

Surprising Your FMCG Customers: A Practical Guide

The FMCG industry, known for its competitive landscape and price sensitivity, can benefit immensely from incorporating surprise into its strategies. Here are some actionable tips:

Surprise in Packaging: Go beyond standard packaging with hidden compartments, augmented reality experiences, or even personalized messages printed on products.

Unexpected Bundles: Offer limited-edition product bundles with surprise items or free samples, encouraging discovery and trial.

Gamification & Loyalty Programs: Reward customers with surprise points, hidden discounts, or exclusive challenges within loyalty programs, driving engagement and repeat purchases.

Social Media Contests & Giveaways: Host interactive contests with unexpected prizes like personalized product hampers or celebrity meet-and-greets, fostering community and brand advocacy.

Seasonal Delights: Offer limited-edition flavors, surprise gifts with seasonal purchases, or special packaging during festivals, tapping into emotional connections and creating buzz.

Personalized Offers & Experiences: Utilize data analytics to offer surprise discounts, birthday gifts, or product recommendations based on individual preferences, fostering a sense of being valued.

Partner with Influencers: Collaborate with social media influencers to create surprise unboxing videos, product reviews, or challenges, leveraging their reach and credibility.

Employee Initiatives: Empower employees to offer small gestures of surprise like handwritten notes, free samples, or upgrades, creating a memorable customer experience.

Charity Partnerships: Partner with local charities and offer surprise donations based on customer purchases, aligning with their values and building goodwill.

Data-Driven Optimization: Track the impact of surprise initiatives through customer feedback, sales data, and social media engagement, iterating and refining your approach for maximum effectiveness.

The key to successful surprise marketing is authenticity and genuine delight. Avoid gimmicks that feel forced or inauthentic, and focus on creating surprises that resonate with your target audience and align with your brand values. By strategically surprising your customers, you can create deeper connections, drive sales, and create a loyal customer base in the competitive FMCG landscape.

A well-placed surprise can be the spark that ignites customer loyalty and brand advocacy. Start incorporating unexpected value into your FMCG strategy today and witness the transformational power of delight.

17. Taste Test: Savor Before you Commit

In the digital age, where convenience reigns supreme, winning over customers can be a challenge. Standing out in a crowded marketplace requires innovative strategies that tap into the inherent human desire for experience and personalization. This is where the "Taste Before You Buy" policy, also known as "Try Before You Purchase," emerges as a powerful tool for online businesses.

This customer-centric approach allows potential buyers to sample a product or service before committing to a full purchase. By removing the fear of the unknown, it fosters trust, encourages exploration, and ultimately leads to increased sales and customer satisfaction.

The Power of Tasting: Building Trust and Driving Conversions

The human experience is driven by sensory engagement. Tasting, touching, or trying something firsthand creates a deeper connection and understanding compared to simply viewing pictures or reading descriptions. This experiential element translates beautifully into the online world through "Taste Before You Buy" policies. Let's explore some key benefits:

Reduced Purchase Anxiety: Consumers often hesitate before buying online due to concerns about product quality, fit, or functionality. "Taste Before You Buy" alleviates these anxieties by allowing them to try the product beforehand, leading to more confident purchase decisions.

Personalized Product Discovery: This policy empowers customers to explore different options and find products that truly resonate with their individual needs and preferences. This personalized discovery leads to higher purchase satisfaction and brand loyalty.

Boost Brand Confidence: By offering "Taste Before You Buy," businesses demonstrate confidence in their offerings. This instills trust in potential customers and positions the brand as transparent and customer-centric.

Increased Customer Engagement: The interactive nature of this policy encourages exploration and experimentation, leading to higher engagement with the brand and its products. This deeper engagement fosters stronger customer relationships.

Valuable Customer Insights: Feedback gathered through "Taste Before You Buy" programs provides valuable insights into customer preferences and can be used to improve product development, marketing strategies, and overall customer experience.

Indian Brands Embracing the "Taste Before You Buy" Trend:

Several Indian brands across diverse industries have successfully implemented "Taste Before You Buy" policies, reaping significant benefits:

Lenskart: This eyewear brand allows customers to try on multiple pairs of glasses at home before purchasing. This helped them overcome the challenge of virtual try-on limitations and led to a significant increase in sales.

Myntra: This fashion e-commerce platform offers a "Try & Buy" policy for select clothing items. Customers can order multiple sizes and styles, try them on at home, and only pay for what they keep. This has driven engagement and boosted conversion rates.

Mamaearth: This natural personal care brand offers sample-sized versions of its products, allowing customers to experience the quality and efficacy before committing to full-size purchases. This strategy has contributed to its rapid growth and customer loyalty.

Urban Company: This home services platform offers a "Satisfaction Guarantee", allowing customers to reschedule or get a refund if they're not happy with the service. This builds trust and encourages first-time users to try their services.

Pepperfry: This furniture e-commerce platform allows customers to visualize furniture in their homes using augmented reality technology. This immersive experience reduces concerns about size and fit, leading to higher conversion rates.

Crafting a Successful "Taste Before You Buy" Strategy for Online Businesses:

Implementing a "Taste Before You Buy" policy requires careful planning and execution. Here are some key guidelines for online businesses:

Select the Right Products: Not all products are suitable for this policy. Start with high-margin items or those facing purchase hesitations due to concerns about fit, quality, or functionality.

Define Clear Terms and Conditions: Establish clear guidelines for the program, including eligibility criteria, return policies, shipping costs, and timeframes for trying the product.

Logistics and Operations: Ensure efficient logistics and reverse logistics processes to handle product returns and exchanges seamlessly.

Communication and Support: Clearly communicate the policy to customers and offer easy-to-use platforms for requesting samples or trials. Provide clear instructions and prompt support throughout the process.

Collect Feedback and Analyze: Gather customer feedback on their experience with the program and use it to refine your offerings and improve the overall customer experience.

Beyond the Initial Bite: "Taste Before You Buy" is not a one-time tactic; it's a cornerstone of a customer-centric approach. Leverage the data and insights gathered to create personalized recommendations, improve product offerings, and build long-term loyalty. Continuously refine your program based on customer feedback and industry trends to remain competitive and provide an exceptional customer experience.

18. Urgency Thrive: The Power of Now

In today's fast-paced world, attention spans are shrinking, and consumers are bombarded with choices. This is where the power of urgency comes in. By creating a sense of scarcity or limited availability, businesses can nudge customers towards making decisions quicker and increase their chances of securing sales.

Understanding the Psychology Behind Urgency

The human brain is wired to respond to perceived threats and opportunities. When presented with a limited-time offer or a product in short supply, our desire to avoid missing out and our fear of regret kick in. This psychological phenomenon, known as FOMO (Fear of Missing Out), motivates us to act swiftly and secure the deal before it's gone.

Scarcity and urgency also trigger a sense of exclusivity, making the product or offer even more desirable. We tend to value things that are perceived as rare or difficult to obtain, leading to increased demand and willingness to pay a premium.

How Big Brands in India Use Urgency to Drive Sales

Several Indian brands have mastered the art of using urgency to drive sales and engagement. Here are five examples:

Flipkart's "Big Billion Days" and "Big Diwali Sale": These limited-time sales events create a sense of urgency with flash deals, countdown timers, and limited-stock notifications. The excitement and anticipation around these events drive massive traffic and sales for Flipkart.

Myntra's "Flash Sale" and "End of Season Sale": Myntra leverages urgency through time-bound sales with significant discounts. They also use countdown timers and limited-stock indicators to create a sense of scarcity and encourage immediate purchases.

Zomato's "Midnight Madness" and "Super Saving Weekends": These limited-time offers with attractive discounts and free delivery incentivize customers to order within a specific timeframe. Zomato uses push notifications and email marketing to further amplify the urgency.

MakeMyTrip's "Last Minute Deals" and "Flash Sale Hotels": These deals cater to impulsive travelers seeking budget-friendly options. The limited availability and urgency create a sense of excitement and encourage immediate booking decisions.

Amazon's "Deal of the Day" and "Lightning Deals": These daily and hourly deals with significant discounts create a sense of urgency and encourage impulse purchases. Amazon also uses countdown timers and limited-stock notifications to further amplify the effect.

Guidelines for Implementing Urgency in Your Marketing Strategy

While urgency can be a powerful tool, it's important to use it ethically and strategically. Here are some guidelines to follow:

Be transparent: Clearly communicate the timeframe and limitations of your offer. Avoid misleading or deceptive tactics.

Offer real value: Ensure your limited-time offer is genuinely attractive and provides value to customers. Don't rely solely on scarcity to drive sales.

Don't overuse it: Frequent use of urgency can lose its effectiveness and create customer fatigue. Use it strategically for specific campaigns and promotions.

Align with your brand identity: Ensure your urgency tactics are consistent with your brand image and values. Avoid creating a sense of desperation or manipulation.

Personalize the experience: Use data and segmentation to personalize urgency messages and offers based on customer preferences and purchase history.

Track and measure: Monitor the effectiveness of your urgency tactics and adjust your approach based on results.

Beyond Sales: The Broader Impact of Urgency

While urgency is primarily used to drive sales, it can also be effective in:

Building excitement and anticipation: Limited-time events and exclusive offers can generate buzz and excitement around your brand.

Encouraging engagement: Urgency can encourage customers to sign up for newsletters, follow social media channels, or participate in contests.

Driving product adoption: Limited-time trials or early access offers can encourage customers to try new products or services.

The power of urgency is a valuable tool in your marketing arsenal. By understanding the psychology behind it and using it ethically and strategically, you can drive sales, increase engagement, and achieve your marketing goals. It is always better to prioritize genuine value and transparency to build lasting customer relationships.

19. Sales Symphony: Harmonizing Value Exchange

Selling, at its core, is not about pushing products or persuading people to part with their money. It's about a beautiful dance of value exchange, where you offer something of worth that enriches the lives of your customers, and in return, they reward you with their trust and business. Imagine it as a harmonious melody, where each note represents a step in building a meaningful connection.

The Stories of Value:

The Aspiring Musician: Piyali dreams of gigging with a professional band. Her worn-out guitar hinders her potential. Enter Mark, a guitar store owner. He doesn't just sell instruments; he understands Piyali's aspirations. He spends time recommending the perfect guitar, one that fits her budget and style. Piyali walks out, not just with a guitar, but with the confidence to chase her dream. Mark's value exchange: a loyal customer, a positive review, and the joy of making music come alive.

The Busy Entrepreneur: David, a busy entrepreneur, struggles to manage his finances. He stumbles upon Jane, a financial advisor who doesn't just offer investment plans. She listens to his goals, understands his anxieties, and tailors a plan that gives him peace of mind and control. David's value exchange: financial security, loyalty, and potential referrals. Jane's value exchange: a long-term client relationship built on trust.

The Notes of the Symphony:

Identifying Needs: It starts with truly understanding your customer's needs, wants, and pain points. What keeps them up at night? What are their aspirations? Don't sell a product; sell a solution to their unique challenges.

Building Trust: Be transparent, honest, and genuine. Share your expertise, offer valuable information, and listen actively. People buy from those they trust.

Demonstrating Value: Clearly articulate how your product or service improves their lives. Use storytelling, data, and testimonials to paint a vivid picture of the value you offer.

Overcoming Objections: Acknowledge concerns and address them with empathy and clarity. Focus on the benefits, not just the features. Offer options and be willing to negotiate.

Building Relationships: Selling is not a one-time transaction. Nurture relationships, provide excellent customer service, and go the extra mile. Exceed expectations and create advocates for your brand.

Beyond the Melody:

It's not just about individual transactions; it's about creating a win-win ecosystem. When you focus on genuine value exchange, you build communities of loyal customers who become your biggest brand ambassadors. Selling is not a solo performance; it's a collaborative effort where everyone benefits.

So, pick up your instrument, maestro, and join the symphony of value exchange. Compose a melody that resonates with your audience, and watch your business flourish in harmony.

20. Voice2Value: Transforming Feedback into Solutions

In today's competitive landscape, understanding your customers is the cornerstone of success. But mere understanding isn't enough. Listening to their voices – their needs, wants, frustrations, and aspirations – and translating them into actionable insights is the key to unlocking true value. This is where the concept of Voice of Customer (VoC) takes center stage.

VoC encompasses all the methods you use to capture and analyze customer feedback – surveys, interviews, social media monitoring, reviews, and more. It's the raw, unfiltered expression of your customers' experience with your brand, product, or service. But how do you transform this rich data into tangible value that fuels innovation, enhances experiences, and ultimately drives business growth?

Here's where the magic happens:

From Data to Insights:

The first step is extracting meaningful insights from the gathered data. This involves going beyond superficial analysis and identifying recurring themes, patterns, and emotions. Advanced analytics tools can help you segment your customer base, prioritize feedback based on impact, and uncover hidden gems that might otherwise be overlooked.

Translate Insights into Actionable Solutions:

Don't let insights gather dust! Translate them into concrete actions that address your customers' needs and pain points. This could involve:

Product development: Use feedback to identify new features, improve existing ones, or even develop entirely new products based on unmet customer needs.

Customer service: Analyze complaints and suggestions to improve service processes, reduce wait times, and personalize interactions.

Marketing: Leverage customer sentiment to tailor messaging, refine targeting strategies, and create campaigns that resonate deeply.

Pricing: Understand customer willingness to pay and develop pricing models that are fair, competitive, and value-driven.

Prioritize Impactful Solutions:

Not all feedback is created equal. Prioritize solutions based on their potential impact on the business and customers. Consider factors like feasibility, cost, and alignment with your overall strategy. Utilize tools like impact matrices to objectively assess the potential return on investment for each solution.

Develop a Culture of Listening:

VoC isn't a one-time exercise; it's an ongoing process. Embed a culture of listening within your organization by:

Empowering employees to solicit and act on customer feedback.

Creating feedback channels that are easy to access and use for customers.

Regularly communicating back to customers about how their feedback is being used.

Celebrating successes achieved through implementing customer-driven solutions.

Just Focus on value, not just volume. Don't get overwhelmed by the sheer amount of data. Focus on the feedback that has the most potential to create value for your customers and your business.

Action speaks louder than words: Implementing even small changes based on customer feedback demonstrates your commitment to listening and builds trust with your customers.

It's a continuous journey: VoC is an ongoing process, not a destination. Regularly collect and analyze feedback, adapt your strategies, and measure the impact of your actions.

The customers are the most valuable asset you have – listen to them, understand them, and use their voices to chart a course towards shared success.

Book Summary

You have reached the final page, and perhaps a familiar refrain is echoing in your mind: "But this won't work in the real world!" We've all heard it – the excuses of the orthodox salesperson, clinging to outdated tactics and dismissing new ideas with a practiced cynicism.

Let's dismantle those excuses, one by one:

- **"People only care about price."** While price is a factor, it's rarely the deciding one. This book equips you to create value that far surpasses the price tag, leaving customers feeling they received more than they bargained for.
- **"I don't have time to be all touchy-feely."** Building genuine connections doesn't require hours of emotional outpouring. It's about active listening, understanding needs, and offering solutions that make a difference. It's about efficiency, not sentimentality.

- **"My job is to close deals, not be a therapist."** You're selling solutions, not just products. Understanding the emotional drivers behind your customer's needs is crucial for tailoring your approach and making a lasting impact. It's not therapy, it's smart business.
- **"This sounds great, but my manager won't buy it."** Lead by example. Start implementing these principles in your interactions, and the results will speak for themselves. Change doesn't always come from the top down, sometimes it sparks from the ground up.
- **"I'm just not cut out for this touchy-feely stuff."** This isn't about becoming someone you're not. It's about drawing on your own strengths, be it your passion, your expertise, or your genuine desire to help others. Authenticity resonates, and people respond to it.

This isn't just a book about selling; it's about **building relationships, creating value, and making a positive impact**. These are principles that resonate in any sphere of life, from the boardroom to the family dinner table.

So, put aside the excuses. This book isn't a magic bullet, but it's a powerful tool in your arsenal. **Choose to Accept the revolution**, to step beyond the tired tactics and tap into the human connection that drives all successful interactions. **People buy from people they like, respect, and trust.** This book shows you how to become that person, not just in sales, but in life.

The choice is yours: **remain stuck in the cycle of excuses, or revolutionize your approach and unleash your true potential.** The world needs more authentic, value-driven individuals, and this book is your invitation to join that movement.

Close the book, but don't close your mind. The journey to becoming a truly impactful salesperson, a true connector, has just begun.

Additional Disclaimer for "The Art of Selling"

The information and strategies presented in "The Art of Selling" are based on the author's personal experiences, knowledge, and observations gathered over two and a half decades in various professional settings. While the author has strived to provide accurate and insightful information, these views and approaches are intended for informational and educational purposes only.

Please note:

The author makes no claims or guarantees as to the success or applicability of the presented strategies in every situation or for every individual. The effectiveness of any sales approach depends on various factors, including market conditions, target audience, individual skills, and external circumstances.

The author is not responsible for any direct or indirect consequences arising from the implementation of the methods or strategies discussed in this book. It is your responsibility to carefully consider your specific circumstances and seek professional advice when necessary before applying any of the presented methods.

The author encourages readers to consult with qualified professionals for personalized guidance and to adapt the provided information to their specific needs and context.

"The Art of Selling" serves as a springboard for exploration and learning, not a definitive rulebook. Ultimately, the responsibility for sales success lies with the individual practitioner. Please act with due diligence and seek professional help where needed.

Common vs. Unorthodox Sales Practices

#	Common Practice	Unorthodox Practice
1.	Focus on features and benefits.	Focus on solving the customer's specific problem.
2.	Use canned sales pitches.	Tailor your approach to each individual customer.
3.	Close hard and fast.	Build trust and rapport before asking for the sale.
4.	Offer discounts and promotions.	Offer value-added services or unique experiences.
5.	Follow a scripted sales process.	Be flexible and adapt your approach based on the situation.
6.	Talk about yourself and your company.	Focus on the customer's needs and aspirations.
7.	Use manipulative tactics to close the deal.	Offer genuine advice and guidance, even if it doesn't lead to a sale immediately.
8.	Focus on competition and price comparisons.	Highlight the unique value proposition of your product or service.

#	Common Practice	Unorthodox Practice
9.	Cold call potential customers.	Engage with potential customers through social media or content marketing.
10.	Attend industry events to network.	Build relationships with potential customers by joining relevant online communities or forums.
11.	Focus on short-term sales.	Develop long-term relationships with customers and encourage repeat business.
12.	Use email automation for outreach.	Write personalized emails that address the customer's specific needs.
13.	Reliance on traditional advertising.	Leverage influencer marketing or customer testimonials.
14.	Focus on generating leads.	Nurture existing leads and turn them into loyal customers.
15.	Sell on features alone.	Tell compelling stories that connect with the customer emotionally.
16.	Always be selling.	Offer valuable content and insights without asking for anything in return.
17.	Speak at industry conferences.	Create and host your own webinars or workshops to share your expertise.

#	Common Practice	Unorthodox Practice
18.	Focus on sales metrics and quotas.	Focus on customer satisfaction and positive outcomes.
19.	Offer generic product demonstrations.	Personalize product demonstrations to showcase specific customer benefits.
20.	Present solutions in isolation.	Present solutions as part of a holistic offering that addresses the customer's entire ecosystem.
21.	Promise unrealistic results.	Set realistic expectations and under-promise, over-deliver.
22.	Focus on closing the deal.	Focus on building a long-term partnership with the customer.
23.	Prioritize quantity over quality leads.	Prioritize high-quality leads that are a good fit for your product or service.
24.	Use pushy sales tactics.	Present yourself as a trusted advisor and expert.
25.	Focus on short-term wins.	Play the long game and invest in building trust and relationships.
26.	Give up easily on objections.	View objections as opportunities to learn more about the customer's needs.
27.	Focus on product complexity.	Simplify value proposition into easily digestible benefits.

#	Common Practice	Unorthodox Practice
28.	Present data in technical jargon.	Translate data into compelling stories and visuals.
29.	Negotiate aggressively for maximum profit.	Seek win-win solutions that prioritize long-term value for both parties.
30.	Focus on product guarantees.	Emphasize customer experience and problem-solving beyond guarantees.
31.	Focus on individual sales reps.	Build a collaborative sales team that leverages diverse strengths.
32.	Track individual performance metrics only.	Track team performance towards shared goals and celebrate collective wins.
33.	Reward only successful deals.	Recognize effort, learning, and improvement even if they don't lead to immediate sales.
34.	Focus on closing techniques.	Focus on active listening and understanding customer needs.
35.	Overuse follow-up calls and emails.	Create personalized content and engage through less disruptive channels.
36.	Present solutions only when requested.	Proactively identify and present solutions to meet potential customer needs.

#	Common Practice	Unorthodox Practice
37.	Focus on product superiority.	Focus on collaborating with customers to achieve their specific goals.
38.	Treat competition as enemies.	Learn from competitors and collaborate when opportunities arise.
39.	Avoid acknowledging weaknesses.	Transparency about limitations builds trust and allows for customization.
40.	Sell only products or services.	Offer unique experiences and add-on value propositions.
41.	Focus on one-time transactions.	Create subscription models or recurring revenue streams.
42.	Focus on the local market.	Tap into global opportunities with a localized approach.
43.	Focus on traditional pricing models.	Experiment with value-based pricing or outcome-based contracts.
44.	Present solutions in person only.	Leverage virtual tools and remote engagement for convenience and global reach.
45.	Focus on closing calls.	Focus on exceeding expectations after the sale for customer retention.

#	Common Practice	Unorthodox Practice
46.	Measure success solely by revenue.	Measure success by customer satisfaction, loyalty, and positive impact.
47.	Focus on product knowledge alone.	Develop emotional intelligence and strong communication skills.
48.	Focus on individual customer interactions.	Contribute to thought leadership and community building within your industry.
49.	Sell during business hours only.	Be available and responsive to customer needs when they arise.
50.	Follow a fixed sales framework.	Continuously experiment and adapt based on data and customer feedback.

Join My Community

https://community.askpndas.com

Please have a look of the other books in the series, "The Art of Living".

www.ingramcontent.com/pod-product-compliance
Lightning Source LLC
Chambersburg PA
CBHW071054240526
45471CB00015B/1897